Lighthouses

Emma Lawson

BookLeaf Publishing

India | USA | UK

Lighthouses © 2022 Emma Lawson

All rights reserved.

No part of this publication may be reproduced, stored in a retrieval system, or transmitted, in any form or by any means, electronic, mechanical, photocopying, recording or otherwise, without the prior written permission of the presenters.

Emma Lawson asserts the moral right to be identified as author of this work.

Presentation by *BookLeaf Publishing*

Web: www.bookleafpub.com

E-mail: info@bookleafpub.com

ISBN: 9789357613880

First edition 2022

To Molly Jae and Finley James. Mama loves you millions and billions all ways, always xxx.

Gratitude & love to Nathan for his support over the years.

To Chris Lawson, thank you for all you have done for me & my family. I am so blessed to have you in my life. Lots of love x.

To the lighthouses, my eternal love and gratitude for all you be and do. Even on the darkest day, your light will always guide the way.

ACKNOWLEDGEMENT

Thank you to my son Finley James for his enthusiastic support of this book. I finished writing it on his 12th birthday!

Special thanks to BookLeaf Publishing. Please visit their website at www.bookleafpub.com.

PREFACE

The traditional Japanese Haiku is a short form of Poetry, which can be traced back to the 9th century. My poems are based on this beautiful form of Poetry. Conforming to the rule of 17 syllables, arranged in three lines of 5, 7, and 5 syllables respectively. The subject matter of each Haiku was my choice. You will find that it represents a more modern take on this classic and much-loved style of Poetry. Thank you for taking the time to read my book, it has been a joy to create it.

Lighthouses.

The lighthouse shines bright.
It doesn't rush out to each boat,
It stands strong for all.

The Illusion.

Time is a marker,
Of an event in your life.
Time is Illusion.

Compassion.

Compassion is key,
It has the power to heal.
Compassion unites.

Balm of love.

Know love never dies,
Souls and love are eternal.
Peace is found through love.

The Golden Ticket.

Believe it or not,
You chose to be here on Earth.
So enjoy your life!

The power of silence.

Silence is power.
Silence takes strength and courage,
To be with yourself.

Angels.

You're never alone,
You're seen, heard, loved, supported.
Breathe and feel we're here.

Ascension process tips.

Remember two things,
Ground and heart centre yourself.
Then life will just flow.

Future healthcare.

Sound and light healing.
The frequencies shift and move,
All that needs to heal.

The whole picture.

Right, wrong and up, down,
Dualistic universe.
Sides of the same coin.

To whom the ancestors call.

Is it just madness?
Can they really be heard?
Witches burned no more.

Record Keeper.

The Akashic realm.
All that is, was and will be.
Stored for you and me.

Heartfelt.

Your powerful heart.
Overunity device.
Creator of life.

Forgiveness for yourself and others.

Forgiveness helps you.
Holding a hot coal burns you,
Forgive and let go.

Home is where the heart is.

Find your way back home.
To the space inside your heart.
All you need is there.

The contrast of life.

Without the darkness,
No gratitude for the light.
Our lives need contrast.

Magic abounds.

Magic surrounds us,
In earth, fire, air and water.
Can you feel the call?

Let bygones be bygones.

Let's release the past.
Now, is where your power lies,
To create the new.

Who am I?

Service to others,
Is the core of who I am.
Highest good of all.

Gratitude is the attitude.

Gratitude creates,
Wellbeing and abundance.
Grateful hearts will thrive.

The recipe for creating.

Thoughts are electric,
Your feelings are magnetic.
Frequency to form.

www.ingramcontent.com/pod-product-compliance
Lightning Source LLC
LaVergne TN
LVHW050249200726
843509LV00015B/2956